Intimate Relationship

HANDBOOK

Navigating Intimacy By Building Trust and Managing Conflict in Close Relationships

Intimate Relationship HANDBOOK

Navigating Intimacy By Building Trust and
Managing Conflict in Close Relationships

Intimate Relationship Handbook:
Navigating Intimacy By Building Trust and Managing Conflict in Close Relationships
1st Edition. 2024 v1.1

ASIN: B0DF6BW31W (Amazon Kindle)
ISBN: 9798338838365 (Amazon Paperback)

TRADEMARKS

Table of Contents

Introduction

The Art of Cultivating Intimacy

Welcome to the beginning of a transformative journey—a journey that will guide you through the intricate dance of intimacy, where connection, trust, and understanding converge to create the foundation of a thriving relationship. As an intimate relationship coach, I have spent years working with couples and individuals who seek to deepen their bonds, overcome challenges, and embrace the full potential of their relationships. This book is a culmination of those experiences, distilled into actionable insights and strategies that you can apply to your own life.

Why Relationships Matter

In the tapestry of life, our relationships are the threads that weave together our experiences, emotions, and growth. Whether romantic, familial, or platonic, relationships form the core of our existence. Yet, despite their importance, many of us navigate these connections without the tools or understanding necessary to nurture them fully. We often find ourselves repeating patterns, struggling with communication, or feeling disconnected from those we care about most. This book is here to change that.

The Promise of This Book

This is not just another book on relationships—it's a guide, a mentor, and a companion on your path to creating a deep, fulfilling, and lasting connection with your partner. Drawing from my extensive experience as a coach, the pages that follow will offer you practical tools, reflective exercises, and powerful strategies to help you navigate the complexities of intimacy. Whether you are in the early stages of a relationship, facing challenges, or simply looking to strengthen your bond, this book is designed to meet you where you are and help you move forward with confidence.

Understanding the Dynamics of Intimacy

Intimacy is often misunderstood as merely a physical connection. While physical intimacy is important, true intimacy encompasses much more. It is the emotional, psychological, and spiritual connection that allows two individuals to fully see and be seen by one another. It is the trust that builds over time, the communication that deepens understanding, and the shared goals that create a sense of unity. This book will explore these dimensions of intimacy in depth, offering you the insights needed to cultivate a relationship that is not just enduring, but truly enriching.

Your Journey Begins Here

Every relationship is unique, and there is no one-size-fits-all solution. However, the principles and practices you will discover in this book are universally applicable. They are rooted in the belief that with the right knowledge, tools, and mindset, every couple can create a relationship that thrives. As you turn the pages, I encourage you to approach each chapter with an open mind and a willingness to reflect on your own experiences. Your journey to a deeper, more fulfilling relationship starts now.

Let's begin.

Communication

In the realm of intimate relationships, communication is not merely an exchange of words; it is the very lifeblood that sustains and nurtures the connection between partners. Effective communication goes beyond the surface level—it involves understanding, empathy, and the ability to connect deeply with your partner's thoughts and emotions. When communication flourishes, relationships thrive. When it falters, even the strongest bonds can weaken.

The Foundation of Effective Communication

At its core, communication is the bridge that connects two individuals, allowing them to share their inner worlds. It is through this bridge that love, trust, and understanding are conveyed. However, communication is not just about speaking; it is equally about listening—truly listening, with an open heart and mind.

1. Active Listening: The Key to Connection

Active listening is perhaps the most important skill in any relationship. It involves fully engaging with your partner's words, emotions, and non-verbal cues, without the distraction of forming a response or judgment. When you listen actively, you create a space where your partner feels heard, understood, and valued. This type of listening is an act of love—it shows that you care deeply about your partner's thoughts and feelings.

Practical Exercise: Next time your partner speaks, focus entirely on their words and emotions. Resist the urge to interrupt or offer advice. Instead, reflect back what you've heard by summarising or asking clarifying questions. Notice how this deepens your connection and understanding.

2. The Art of Expressing Yourself

Just as listening is crucial, so is the ability to express yourself clearly and authentically. In intimate relationships, open expression of thoughts, feelings, and needs is essential for building trust and closeness. However, expressing yourself requires more than just speaking your mind—it involves doing so in a way that is respectful, clear, and mindful of your partner's feelings.

Practical Tip: Use "I" statements to communicate your feelings and needs without blaming or accusing. For example, instead of saying, "You never listen to me," try, "I feel unheard when I'm speaking and it seems like you're distracted." This shifts the conversation from a place of conflict to one of understanding and collaboration.

3. Non-Verbal Communication: The Unspoken Language

Communication in relationships is not limited to words. Much of what we convey to our partners is expressed through non-verbal cues—body language, facial expressions, eye contact, and tone of voice. These signals can either reinforce what we say or contradict it, making it essential to be aware of the messages we send without speaking.

Practical Exercise: Pay attention to your non-verbal communication. During your next conversation, observe your posture, gestures, and facial expressions. Are they aligned with your words? Practice maintaining open and relaxed body language, making eye contact, and using a warm tone to enhance your verbal messages.

4. Navigating Difficult Conversations

Every relationship encounters moments of tension or disagreement, and how you communicate during these times can make all the difference. Navigating difficult conversations requires patience, empathy, and a willingness to see things from your partner's perspective. It's important to approach these conversations with the intent to understand and resolve, rather than to win or be right.

Practical Tip: Set aside a specific time to discuss sensitive topics, ensuring that both you and your partner are in a calm and receptive state of mind. Begin the conversation with a positive statement or acknowledgment, then gently introduce the issue. Use phrases like "I've noticed" or "I feel concerned about" rather than making accusations.

5. The Power of Validation

Validation is the process of acknowledging and accepting your partner's feelings, even if you don't necessarily agree with them. It's a way of showing empathy and respect for their emotional experience, which can significantly enhance your connection and reduce conflict.

Practical Exercise: The next time your partner expresses an emotion or concern, validate their feelings by saying something like, "I can see why you would feel that way," or "That sounds really challenging." Validation doesn't mean you agree with everything your partner says; it means you recognize their right to their feelings.

The Ongoing Journey of Communication

Effective communication is not a one-time achievement; it's an ongoing practice that evolves as your relationship grows. As you deepen your understanding of each other, your communication skills will naturally develop. Remember, the goal is not perfection, but progress—every effort you make to communicate more effectively brings you closer to a more intimate, fulfilling relationship.

Reflective Questions

At the end of this chapter, take a moment to reflect on your communication patterns:

1. How often do you practice active listening with your partner?
2. Are there areas in your relationship where communication tends to break down? What can you do to improve these areas?

3. How do you express your needs and emotions? Are there ways to do this more effectively?
4. What non-verbal cues do you notice in yourself and your partner during conversations?
5. How do you handle difficult conversations? What strategies can you implement to navigate these better?

Communication is the cornerstone of any successful relationship. By committing to improving how you listen, express yourself, and navigate conversations, you lay the groundwork for a deeper, more meaningful connection with your partner. This chapter offers tools to help you on that journey, but remember that the true power of communication lies in your willingness to continually practice and refine these skills. Together, you can build a relationship that not only survives but thrives on the strength of your shared understanding and connection.

Building Trust and Honesty

Building trust and honesty in an intimate relationship is a delicate yet vital process that forms the very foundation of a strong and enduring connection. These two elements intertwine, creating a tapestry of transparency, reliability, and emotional security. Let's delve into why cultivating trust and honesty is essential for the flourishing of an intimate relationship.

Trust and honesty are the bedrock of any enduring intimate relationship. Without them, even the most passionate connection can crumble under the weight of insecurity and doubt. Building and maintaining trust, alongside practicing honesty, are not one-time efforts but ongoing commitments that require intention, consistency, and vulnerability. In this chapter, we will explore how to cultivate these essential pillars in your relationship, ensuring that your bond remains resilient and deeply fulfilling.

Understanding Trust: The Foundation of Emotional Safety

Trust is the assurance that you can rely on your partner emotionally, physically, and psychologically. It is the confidence that your partner will be there for you, even when times are tough. This foundation of emotional safety allows for vulnerability, intimacy, and the mutual support that sustains a long-term relationship.

1. Consistency: The Key to Trustworthiness

Trust is built through consistent actions over time. It's not grand gestures but the everyday reliability that solidifies trust. When your words and actions align consistently, your partner learns that they can depend on you. This reliability forms the threads of trust that weave a secure and stable connection.

Practical Exercise: Reflect on the promises you've made to your partner, big or small. Are you consistently following through on them? Identify one area where you could be more reliable and commit to making a small, positive change. Over time, these consistent actions will strengthen the trust in your relationship.

2. Vulnerability: The Courage to Be Open

True honesty in a relationship requires vulnerability—the courage to reveal your true self, including your fears, insecurities, and flaws. When you are vulnerable, you invite your partner to see and accept you as you are, which deepens the emotional bond between you. Vulnerability is not a sign of weakness; it is a powerful tool that builds trust and fosters intimacy.

Practical Tip: Share something with your partner that you've been hesitant to discuss. It could be a fear, a regret, or a past experience. Approach the conversation with an open heart, and invite your partner to do the same. This mutual vulnerability will help build a deeper level of trust.

The Role of Honesty: Creating Transparency in Your Relationship

Honesty is the backbone of trust. It involves being truthful with your partner, even when the truth is difficult to share or hear. Honesty fosters transparency, which is crucial for building and maintaining trust over the long term.

3. Practicing Radical Honesty

Radical honesty is about being fully transparent in your relationship. It doesn't mean being harsh or blunt but rather being open about your thoughts, feelings, and actions. Practicing radical honesty requires you to communicate openly with your partner, even about things that might cause discomfort or conflict. By doing so, you prevent misunderstandings and build a relationship grounded in truth.

Practical Exercise: Identify a topic you've been avoiding with your partner, perhaps out of fear of conflict or discomfort. Approach this conversation with the intent to be fully honest, while also being compassionate and understanding. Notice how this honesty impacts your connection and trust.

4. Addressing Mistakes with Accountability

No one is perfect, and mistakes are inevitable in any relationship. What matters is how you address these mistakes. Taking responsibility for your actions, apologizing sincerely, and making amends are critical steps in rebuilding trust after it's been damaged. Accountability shows your partner that you respect them and value the trust they place in you.

Practical Tip: The next time you make a mistake, own it without deflecting or making excuses. Apologize sincerely and discuss with your partner how you can avoid repeating the mistake in the future. This approach not only repairs trust but also strengthens it.

The Ongoing Work of Trust and Honesty

Trust and honesty are not static; they require ongoing attention and effort. Just as a garden needs regular care to flourish, so too does your relationship need continuous nurturing. By committing to consistency, vulnerability, and transparency, you create a strong foundation that can weather the inevitable challenges of life.

Reflective Questions

As you work to build and maintain trust and honesty in your relationship, consider the following questions:

In what ways do you consistently demonstrate reliability in your relationship?

- » How comfortable are you with being vulnerable with your partner?
- » What steps can you take to increase this comfort?

- » Are there areas where you feel hesitant to be fully honest? Why?
- » How can you address this hesitancy?
- » How do you handle mistakes in your relationship?
- » Are there ways you could be more accountable?

Trust and honesty are the pillars upon which a strong, healthy relationship is built. They provide the safety and transparency needed for both partners to feel secure, valued, and loved. By practicing consistency, embracing vulnerability, and committing to radical honesty, you will not only build trust but also create a relationship that is rich in depth, connection, and mutual respect. Remember, the work of building trust and honesty is ongoing, but the rewards—a deep, enduring relationship—are well worth the effort.

Managing Conflict

Conflict is an inevitable part of any relationship. How you manage conflict, however, determines whether it becomes a destructive force or a catalyst for growth. When approached with care and intention, conflicts can deepen understanding, strengthen bonds, and lead to greater intimacy. In this chapter, we will explore strategies to manage conflict effectively, ensuring that it serves as a stepping stone rather than a stumbling block in your relationship.

Understanding the Nature of Conflict

Conflict often arises when two individuals, each with their own perspectives, needs, and experiences, encounter a situation where these elements clash. It's important to understand that conflict is not inherently negative. In fact, it can be a powerful opportunity to address underlying issues, clarify expectations, and foster mutual respect. The key lies in how you approach and navigate these moments of tension.

1. Shifting Your Mindset: Viewing Conflict as a Growth Opportunity

The first step in managing conflict is to shift your mindset. Instead of viewing conflict as something to avoid or fear, see it as an opportunity for growth. Conflict can be a doorway to deeper understanding and connection if approached with the right attitude. This shift in perspective allows you to engage in conflicts with a sense of curiosity and openness rather than defensiveness or anger.

Practical Tip: Next time you find yourself in a conflict with your partner, take a moment to pause and reframe the situation. Ask yourself, "What can I learn from this?" and "How can this conflict bring us closer together?" This mindset shift will help you approach the conversation with a more constructive and positive attitude.

The Essentials of Constructive Conflict Resolution

Constructive conflict resolution is about addressing issues directly while maintaining respect and empathy for your partner. It involves clear communication, active listening, and a commitment to finding solutions that work for both partners.

2. Active Listening: Truly Hearing Your Partner

Active listening is the cornerstone of effective conflict resolution. It involves fully focusing on your partner's words, emotions, and underlying concerns without interrupting or preparing your rebuttal. When you listen actively, you create a space where your partner feels heard and understood, which is crucial for resolving conflict.

Practical Exercise: During your next conflict, practice active listening by giving your full attention to your partner. Reflect back what you've heard to ensure you understand their perspective, and ask clarifying questions if needed. This not only defuses tension but also paves the way for a more productive conversation.

3. The Power of "I" Statements: Communicating Without Blame

Using "I" statements is an effective way to express your feelings and needs without blaming or accusing your partner. Instead of saying, "You never listen to me," try, "I feel frustrated when I don't feel heard." This approach helps you take responsibility for your emotions while also inviting your partner to understand your perspective without feeling attacked.

Practical Tip: Practice reframing your concerns into "I" statements before bringing them up during a conflict. This not only reduces defensiveness but also encourages a more empathetic and open dialogue.

4. Finding Common Ground: The Art of Compromise

At the heart of successful conflict resolution is the ability to find common ground. Compromise is not about one person winning or losing but about both partners working together to find a solution that respects each other's needs and values. It's about being willing to give a little to gain a lot in the relationship.

Practical Exercise: In your next disagreement, focus on finding a solution that honors both your needs. Identify areas where you can be flexible and where your partner can compromise. The goal is to reach a resolution that both of you can feel good about, strengthening your bond in the process.

5. Timing and Environment: Choosing the Right Moment

When it comes to conflict resolution, timing and environment matter. Addressing sensitive issues in the heat of the moment or in a stressful environment can escalate the conflict. Instead, choose a time when both of you are calm and can focus on the conversation without distractions.

Practical Tip: If a conflict arises at a bad time, agree to pause the conversation and set a specific time to revisit it when you're both in a better state of mind. This shows respect for each other's emotional space and ensures that the conversation will be more constructive.

Navigating Common Sources of Conflict

While conflicts can arise from many different sources, some areas tend to be particularly challenging in relationships. Understanding these common triggers can help you address them proactively.

6. Communication Breakdown

Miscommunication is a frequent source of conflict. Whether it's unclear expectations, misunderstandings, or a lack of communication, these issues can create frustration and resentment. Addressing communication breakdowns involves being clear, direct, and ensuring that both partners are on the same page.

Practical Exercise: Regularly check in with your partner about how you communicate. Are there areas where messages are getting lost or misinterpreted? How can you both improve the clarity and effectiveness of your communication?

7. Differences in Values and Beliefs

Partners may have different values, beliefs, or approaches to life that can lead to conflict. These differences don't have to be divisive if handled with respect and understanding. The key is to acknowledge these differences and find ways to coexist harmoniously.

Practical Tip: When differences arise, engage in open dialogue to explore each other's perspectives. Seek to understand rather than change your partner's values, and look for ways to honor both viewpoints within the relationship.

8. Financial Stress

Money is a common source of tension in relationships. Differing attitudes towards spending, saving, or financial planning can lead to conflicts. Addressing financial stress involves open and honest discussions about money, setting shared goals, and creating a plan that works for both partners.

Practical Exercise: Set aside time to discuss your financial goals and concerns with your partner. Create a budget together that reflects both of your priorities and commit to regular financial check-ins to ensure you're on track.

Transforming Conflict into Connection

Every conflict holds the potential to either drive a wedge between you or bring you closer together. By approaching conflicts with empathy, openness, and a willingness to grow, you can transform these challenges into opportunities to deepen your connection and understanding.

Reflective Questions

As you work on managing conflict in your relationship, consider these questions:

1. How do you typically react during a conflict? Are there patterns you'd like to change?
2. What strategies have been most effective in resolving past conflicts with your partner?
3. How can you approach future conflicts with a mindset of growth and understanding?
4. Are there any unresolved conflicts in your relationship that need to be addressed?

Managing conflict is an essential skill for any lasting relationship. By embracing conflict as an opportunity for growth, practicing active listening, and seeking solutions that honor both partners, you can turn moments of tension into stepping stones toward a stronger, more resilient connection. Remember, it's not the absence of conflict that defines a healthy relationship, but how you handle it together that truly matters.

Financial Planning Together

Money is one of the most significant factors in any relationship, yet it is often the source of misunderstandings, stress, and conflict. Financial planning together is not just about managing money; it's about aligning your values, goals, and dreams as a couple. When approached with openness and collaboration, financial planning can strengthen your relationship and pave the way for a secure and harmonious future.

The Importance of Financial Unity

Financial unity is about more than just pooling resources; it's about creating a shared vision for your future together. Whether you're navigating daily expenses, saving for major milestones, or planning for retirement, being on the same page financially ensures that both partners feel secure, respected, and invested in the relationship.

1. Aligning Financial Values and Goals

The first step in successful financial planning is aligning your financial values and goals. Each person brings their own set of beliefs, habits, and expectations about money, shaped by their upbringing and experiences. It's crucial to have open discussions about what money means to each of you and how you envision your financial future.

Practical Exercise: Set aside time to discuss your individual financial values and long-term goals. What are your priorities—saving, spending, investing, or paying off debt? How do you envision your financial future together? Write down your shared goals and create a plan to achieve them, ensuring that both partners' values are reflected in the process.

2. Creating a Collaborative Budget

A budget is a powerful tool that helps you manage your money effectively and avoid unnecessary stress. However, a budget should be a collaborative effort, reflecting the needs, desires, and responsibilities of both partners. It's about creating a financial plan that allows you to live comfortably while working towards your shared goals.

Practical Tip: Develop a joint budget that includes all income, expenses, savings, and investments. Be transparent about your individual spending habits and work together to allocate funds in a way that meets both your needs and long-term goals. Regularly review and adjust the budget as your circumstances and priorities evolve.

3. Communicating Openly About Money

Open and honest communication is the foundation of any successful financial plan. Many couples avoid discussing money because it can be uncomfortable or lead to conflict. However, avoiding these conversations only leads to misunderstandings and resentment. By discussing finances openly and regularly, you build trust and ensure that both partners are on the same page.

Practical Exercise: Schedule regular financial check-ins, where you discuss your current financial situation, upcoming expenses, and any concerns you might have. Use these conversations to celebrate your financial successes, address challenges, and make any necessary adjustments to your plan. The key is to approach these discussions with a spirit of collaboration and mutual respect.

4. Navigating Financial Challenges Together

Every relationship will face financial challenges at some point—whether it's dealing with debt, managing unexpected expenses, or navigating a change in income. The way you handle these challenges together can either strengthen your relationship or create tension. It's important to approach financial difficulties as a team, working together to find solutions that work for both partners.

Practical Tip: When faced with a financial challenge, take a step back and assess the situation together. Identify the problem, discuss possible solutions, and decide on a plan of action that you both can commit to. Remember, it's not about who's right or wrong, but about finding a way forward that preserves the harmony in your relationship.

5. Planning for the Future: Saving and Investing Together

Financial planning isn't just about managing the present; it's also about securing your future. Whether you're saving for a home, planning for retirement, or building an emergency fund, having a clear and shared vision for your financial future is crucial. Investing in your future together not only provides financial security but also strengthens your commitment to each other.

Practical Exercise: Set financial goals for the short, medium, and long term. Determine how much you need to save or invest each month to reach these goals, and decide on the best strategies for achieving them. Whether it's contributing to retirement accounts, saving for a down payment, or investing in the stock market, make sure you're both informed and involved in the decision-making process.

Balancing Individual and Joint Finances

While financial unity is important, it's also essential to respect each partner's need for financial autonomy. Balancing individual and joint finances allows each partner to maintain a sense of independence while contributing to the shared financial goals of the relationship.

6. Maintaining Financial Autonomy Within a Partnership

Maintaining separate accounts for personal expenses can help avoid conflicts over discretionary spending and provide a sense of financial independence. However, it's important to ensure that these individual financial decisions don't undermine your joint goals.

Practical Tip: Consider setting up a system where each partner contributes a set amount to a joint account for shared expenses, while maintaining separate accounts for personal spending. This allows you to manage your finances together while also respecting each other's autonomy.

7. Preparing for Life's Transitions

Life is full of transitions—marriage, buying a home, starting a family, or retiring. Each of these milestones brings with it a new set of financial challenges and opportunities. Preparing for these transitions together ensures that you can navigate them smoothly and with confidence.

Practical Exercise: Discuss potential life transitions that you may face in the coming years. How will these changes impact your financial situation, and what steps can you take now to prepare? Whether it's saving for a child's education, planning for a career change, or setting up a retirement plan, proactive planning helps you face the future with certainty.

Building a Legacy Together

Financial planning is not just about the here and now; it's also about the legacy you want to leave behind. Whether it's providing for your children, supporting causes you care about, or ensuring each other's financial security, your financial plan should reflect the values and aspirations you share as a couple.

8. Discussing Long-Term Plans and Legacy Goals

Talking about the future can be daunting, but it's essential for ensuring that your long-term goals are aligned. Whether you're thinking about retirement, estate planning, or philanthropic efforts, having these discussions early and regularly helps you create a lasting legacy together.

Practical Tip: Create a vision board together that represents your long-term financial goals and legacy. Use it as a visual reminder of what you're working towards and revisit it regularly to ensure you're on track. This not only keeps you focused on your goals but also reinforces your commitment to building a future together.

Reflective Questions

As you work on financial planning together, consider the following questions:

> » How well do our financial values and goals align?
> » Are there areas in our budget where we could improve our collaboration?
> » How can we communicate more openly and effectively about money?
> » What financial challenges are we currently facing, and how can we address them as a team?
> » How are we preparing for our future, both individually and as a couple?

Financial planning together is a journey that requires trust, communication, and a shared vision for the future. By aligning your financial values, creating a collaborative budget, and preparing for life's transitions, you can build a secure and harmonious future together. Remember, the strength of your relationship is not determined by the absence of financial challenges, but by how you navigate them as a united team. Together, you can create a financial plan that not only secures your future but also enriches your relationship every step of the way.

Intimacy and Physical Connection

Intimacy is the heartbeat of any romantic relationship. It is the sacred space where emotional connection and physical affection meet, creating a bond that transcends the ordinary. Intimacy isn't just about the physical act of connecting; it's about the depth of emotional closeness and the mutual understanding that forms the foundation of a thriving relationship. In this chapter, we will explore how to nurture both emotional and physical intimacy, ensuring that your relationship remains vibrant, connected, and deeply fulfilling.

The Many Facets of Intimacy

Intimacy in a relationship is multifaceted. It encompasses emotional, physical, intellectual, and spiritual dimensions, each contributing to the overall connection between partners. While physical intimacy often gets the most attention, emotional intimacy is equally, if not more, important. It's the emotional bond that sustains a relationship, especially during challenging times.

1. Emotional Intimacy: The Foundation of Connection

Emotional intimacy is the bedrock of a close and fulfilling relationship. It involves being open, vulnerable, and fully present with your partner. When emotional intimacy is strong, physical intimacy becomes a natural extension of the emotional bond. Cultivating emotional intimacy requires ongoing effort, trust, and a willingness to share your innermost thoughts and feelings.

Practical Exercise: Set aside time each week to engage in deep, meaningful conversations with your partner. Ask open-ended questions that encourage them to share their thoughts, dreams, and feelings. Listen actively and respond with empathy. This practice not only strengthens your emotional bond but also enhances the overall intimacy in your relationship.

2. Physical Intimacy: More Than Just Physicality

Physical intimacy is not solely about sexual activity—it encompasses all forms of physical touch that express love, care, and connection. Holding hands, hugging, kissing, and even a gentle touch on the arm can communicate warmth and affection. Physical intimacy is a powerful way to reinforce your emotional bond and keep the connection alive.

Practical Tip: Make a conscious effort to incorporate more non-sexual physical touch into your daily interactions. Simple gestures like a kiss on the forehead, a warm hug, or holding hands while walking can significantly enhance the feeling of closeness and connection in your relationship.

3. Understanding Each Other's Intimacy Needs

Every individual has different needs and preferences when it comes to intimacy. Understanding and respecting these differences is key to maintaining a healthy and satisfying physical connection. Open communication about your needs and desires is essential, as is being attuned to your partner's needs.

Practical Exercise: Have an open and honest conversation with your partner about your intimacy needs. Discuss what makes you feel connected, loved, and fulfilled, and encourage your partner to share the same. This dialogue helps you both understand each other's preferences and find ways to meet each other's needs more effectively.

The Role of Communication in Intimacy

Communication is the cornerstone of both emotional and physical intimacy. Without clear and open communication, misunderstandings and unmet needs can create distance between partners. By communicating openly about your desires, boundaries, and feelings, you create a safe space where intimacy can flourish.

4. Expressing Your Desires and Boundaries

Healthy intimacy requires that both partners feel comfortable expressing their desires and setting boundaries. This involves being honest about what you enjoy, what you're curious about, and what you're not comfortable with. Respecting each other's boundaries is crucial for maintaining trust and ensuring that physical intimacy remains a positive and fulfilling experience.

Practical Tip: Initiate a conversation with your partner about your physical relationship. Share your desires and boundaries, and invite your partner to do the same. Approach the conversation with curiosity and a willingness to listen, ensuring that both of you feel heard and respected.

5. Navigating Differences in Intimacy Preferences

It's common for partners to have different levels of desire or preferences when it comes to physical intimacy. These differences don't have to create conflict; instead, they can be an opportunity to explore new ways of connecting. The key is to approach these differences with understanding and a collaborative mindset.

Practical Exercise: If you and your partner have differing intimacy preferences, consider finding a middle ground. Discuss ways to meet each other's needs without pressure or resentment. For example, if one partner desires more frequent physical intimacy, find ways to increase emotional closeness or non-sexual physical touch, which can enhance overall connection and satisfaction.

Sustaining Intimacy Over Time

Sustaining intimacy in a long-term relationship requires ongoing effort and attention. As life becomes busy with work, family, and other responsibilities, it's easy for intimacy to take a backseat. However, making intimacy a priority is essential for maintaining a strong, connected relationship.

6. Scheduling Time for Intimacy

While spontaneity is often associated with romance, intentionally scheduling time for intimacy can be just as powerful. Setting aside regular time to connect, both emotionally and physically, ensures that intimacy remains a central part of your relationship.

Practical Tip: Set a regular "date night" or "intimacy time" each week where you focus solely on each other. This could involve going out for a romantic dinner, spending quality time at home, or simply having an uninterrupted conversation. The key is to create a space where you can reconnect and nurture your bond.

7. Keeping the Spark Alive

Keeping the spark alive in a long-term relationship involves creativity, effort, and a willingness to try new things. Whether it's exploring new activities together, trying new forms of physical intimacy, or simply being playful and spontaneous, keeping things fresh helps sustain the excitement and connection between you.

Practical Exercise: Try something new together—whether it's a new activity, a weekend getaway, or exploring new ways of being intimate. This shared experience can reignite the spark and bring a renewed sense of excitement to your relationship.

Intimacy as a Journey

Intimacy is not a destination but an ongoing journey that evolves as your relationship grows. It requires continuous nurturing, attention, and effort. By prioritizing both emotional and physical intimacy, you build a relationship that is deeply connected, resilient, and fulfilling.

Reflective Questions

As you work on nurturing intimacy in your relationship, consider the following questions:

- » How emotionally connected do you feel to your partner?
- » What can you do to deepen this connection?
- » Are there aspects of physical intimacy that you'd like to explore or enhance?
- » How well do you communicate your desires and boundaries with your partner?

» What steps can you take to ensure that intimacy remains a priority in your relationship?
» How can you bring more creativity and spontaneity into your intimate life?

Intimacy and physical connection are the threads that weave the fabric of a strong and enduring relationship. By nurturing both emotional and physical intimacy, communicating openly, and making intimacy a priority, you create a bond that is rich, deep, and satisfying. Remember, intimacy is not just about physical closeness—it's about connecting on every level and building a relationship that supports, nurtures, and fulfills both partners. Embrace the journey of intimacy, and let it lead you to an ever-deeper connection with your partner.

Balancing Personal Space and Togetherness

In any intimate relationship, finding the right balance between personal space and togetherness is crucial. Both are essential to a healthy partnership—personal space allows for individual growth and self-care, while togetherness nurtures connection and shared experiences. Striking this balance can be challenging, but when achieved, it creates a relationship that is both deeply connected and individually fulfilling. In this chapter, we'll explore how to harmonize independence and connection, ensuring that both partners feel valued and understood.

The Importance of Personal Space in a Relationship

Personal space is not a sign of distance or disinterest; rather, it is a vital component of a healthy relationship. It allows each partner to maintain their sense of self, pursue personal interests, and recharge emotionally. When personal space is respected and valued, it enhances the overall dynamic of the relationship, making the time spent together more meaningful.

1. Understanding the Need for Personal Space

Every individual has different needs when it comes to personal space. Some may require more time alone to reflect, pursue hobbies, or simply recharge, while others may thrive on constant companionship. It's important to recognize and respect these differences to maintain harmony in the relationship.

Practical Exercise: Reflect on your own needs for personal space. How much time do you need to feel recharged and fulfilled? Have an open conversation with your partner about your needs and encourage them to share theirs. Understanding and respecting each other's preferences can help prevent feelings of suffocation or neglect.

2. Creating Healthy Boundaries

Boundaries are essential for maintaining a balance between personal space and togetherness. These boundaries are not about building walls between you and your partner but about creating a healthy environment where both individuals can thrive. Setting clear boundaries helps ensure that each partner's needs are met without compromising the connection.

Practical Tip: Discuss and agree on boundaries that work for both of you. This might include dedicated time for personal activities, respecting alone time, or setting limits on how much time is spent together. Make sure these boundaries are flexible enough to adapt to changing circumstances while still honoring each partner's needs.

The Power of Togetherness in Building Connection

While personal space is important, so too is the time you spend together. Togetherness strengthens the emotional bond between partners, fosters intimacy, and creates shared memories that form the foundation of your relationship. It's about being present with each other, both physically and emotionally, and enjoying the shared journey.

3. Prioritizing Quality Time

Quality time is not just about being in the same space; it's about engaging with each other in meaningful ways. Whether it's having deep conversations, enjoying shared hobbies, or simply being present without distractions, quality time nurtures the connection and keeps the relationship strong.

Practical Exercise: Identify activities that both you and your partner enjoy and set aside regular time to engage in them together. This could be as simple as a weekly date night, a shared hobby, or even just a dedicated hour each evening to connect without distractions. The goal is to create regular opportunities for meaningful interaction.

4. Balancing Togetherness and Independence

Healthy relationships thrive on a balance between togetherness and independence. While spending time together is crucial, it's equally important to maintain your individuality. A relationship that allows for both personal growth and shared experiences is one that can withstand the test of time.

Practical Tip: Encourage each other to pursue individual interests and goals, while also finding ways to support these pursuits as a couple. Celebrate each other's successes and be there for each other's challenges, all while maintaining a strong, shared connection. This balance ensures that both partners feel fulfilled and supported, both individually and as a couple.

Navigating Common Challenges

Balancing personal space and togetherness can present challenges, especially when partners have differing needs or expectations. These challenges can lead to feelings of neglect, resentment, or suffocation if not addressed openly and constructively.

5. Addressing Differences in Needs

It's common for partners to have different levels of need for personal space or togetherness. These differences don't have to lead to conflict if they are acknowledged and addressed with understanding and compromise.

Practical Exercise: If you and your partner have differing needs, take time to discuss them openly. Find a compromise that allows both of you to feel comfortable and respected. For example, if one partner needs more alone time, agree on specific times when they can have that space, while also ensuring that quality time together is prioritized.

6. Overcoming Feelings of Guilt or Resentment

Sometimes, requesting personal space can lead to feelings of guilt, while a partner's need for space can cause feelings of rejection or resentment. It's important to recognize these emotions and address them constructively.

Practical Tip: If you feel guilty for needing personal space, remind yourself that taking care of your own needs makes you a better partner in the long run. If you feel rejected when your partner requests space, communicate your feelings openly, and seek reassurance from your partner. Understanding each other's perspectives can help alleviate these negative emotions.

The Role of Communication in Balancing Space and Togetherness

Effective communication is key to maintaining a healthy balance between personal space and togetherness. Open, honest dialogue about your needs, boundaries, and feelings helps prevent misunderstandings and ensures that both partners feel valued and respected.

7. Regular Check-Ins

Regular check-ins are a valuable tool for maintaining balance in your relationship. These conversations provide an opportunity to reassess your needs and make any necessary adjustments to your routine.

Practical Exercise: Schedule regular check-ins with your partner to discuss how you're both feeling about the balance between personal space and togetherness. Use these conversations to address any concerns, celebrate what's working well, and make adjustments as needed. This ongoing dialogue helps keep your relationship healthy and balanced.

Creating a Relationship That Supports Both Partners

Ultimately, a healthy relationship supports the needs of both partners. By balancing personal space and togetherness, you create a dynamic where both individuals can grow, thrive, and feel deeply connected. This balance is not static; it evolves as your relationship grows and changes, requiring ongoing attention and care.

Reflective Questions

As you work on balancing personal space and togetherness, consider the following questions:

» How much personal space do you need to feel fulfilled?
» How does this compare to your partner's needs?
» Are there boundaries you could set to better balance your personal space and time together?
» How can you prioritize quality time with your partner, even amidst busy schedules?
» What strategies can you use to navigate differences in your needs for space and togetherness?
» How can regular communication help you maintain a healthy balance in your relationship?

Balancing personal space and togetherness is an ongoing process that requires mutual understanding, respect, and open communication. By recognizing and honoring each other's needs, setting healthy boundaries, and prioritizing quality time together, you can create a relationship that is both deeply connected and individually fulfilling. Remember, the goal is not to find a perfect balance, but to create a dynamic that allows both you and your partner to thrive, both as individuals and as a couple. With attention and care, you can build a relationship that supports and enriches every aspect of your lives together.

Long-Term Relationship Goals

A successful relationship is not just built on love and affection in the present but also on a shared vision for the future. Setting long-term relationship goals is about crafting a path together that aligns with both partners' values, dreams, and aspirations. These goals provide direction and purpose, helping you navigate the journey of life together with clarity and mutual understanding. In this chapter, we'll explore how to set and achieve long-term relationship goals, ensuring that your partnership remains strong, resilient, and fulfilling.

The Importance of a Shared Vision

At the heart of every thriving relationship is a shared vision—a collective sense of purpose that guides your journey together. This vision is not static; it evolves as you grow individually and as a couple. Whether it's building a family, traveling the world, or supporting each other's personal ambitions, having clear long-term goals helps you stay connected and motivated, even when faced with challenges.

1. Identifying Core Values and Joint Aspirations

Before setting long-term goals, it's essential to identify your core values and joint aspirations. These are the principles and dreams that define who you are as individuals and as a couple. Aligning your goals with these core values ensures that your relationship is built on a strong foundation of mutual respect and shared purpose.

Practical Exercise: Sit down together and discuss your individual core values—what matters most to you in life? Next, explore your joint aspirations. What do you want to achieve together in the next five, ten, or twenty years? Write down your shared goals and revisit them regularly to ensure they still resonate with both of you.

2. Setting SMART Relationship Goals

Once you've identified your core values and joint aspirations, the next step is to set specific, measurable, achievable, relevant, and time-bound (SMART) goals. These goals provide a clear roadmap for your relationship, helping you track progress and celebrate successes along the way.

Practical Tip: When setting your long-term relationship goals, make sure they are SMART. For example, instead of setting a vague goal like "We want to travel more," create a SMART goal like "We will visit three new countries together over the next five years." This level of specificity gives you both a clear target to work towards and makes it easier to achieve your goals.

Aligning Individual and Joint Goals

While long-term relationship goals are important, it's also crucial to balance these with your individual aspirations. A healthy relationship supports the growth and fulfillment of both partners, allowing each person to pursue their own dreams while working towards shared goals.

3. Balancing Personal Ambitions with Relationship Goals

In any relationship, there may be times when personal ambitions seem to conflict with joint goals. However, these conflicts don't have to be divisive. With open communication and mutual support, you can find ways to pursue both individual and joint aspirations in harmony.

Practical Exercise: Regularly discuss your personal ambitions with your partner. Are there areas where your individual goals align with your relationship goals? How can you support each other's personal growth while still working towards your shared vision? Look for ways to integrate your personal ambitions into your long-term relationship goals, ensuring that both partners feel fulfilled and valued.

4. Supporting Each Other's Growth

Supporting each other's personal growth is key to maintaining a healthy, long-term relationship. Whether it's pursuing a career change, going back to school, or developing a new hobby, showing genuine interest and encouragement in each other's personal goals strengthens your bond and fosters mutual respect.

Practical Tip: Be proactive in supporting your partner's growth. This might involve helping them find resources, offering emotional support during challenging times, or simply celebrating their successes. By investing in each other's growth, you create a relationship dynamic that is both nurturing and empowering.

Navigating Life's Transitions Together

Life is full of transitions—career changes, relocations, starting a family, or entering retirement. Each of these transitions brings new challenges and opportunities that can impact your long-term goals. Successfully navigating these changes requires flexibility, open communication, and a commitment to your shared vision.

5. Adapting to Change

Change is inevitable, and long-term goals may need to be adjusted as life evolves. Being open to adapting your plans ensures that your goals remain relevant and achievable, even as circumstances change. Flexibility is key to maintaining harmony and forward momentum in your relationship.

Practical Exercise: Regularly review your long-term goals together, especially during significant life transitions. Discuss how these changes might impact your goals and what adjustments need to be made. Whether it's delaying a plan, shifting priorities, or setting new goals altogether, approaching these changes with flexibility and a positive mindset will help keep your relationship on track.

6. Building Resilience Together

Resilience is the ability to bounce back from setbacks and challenges, both as individuals and as a couple. Building resilience together involves fostering a strong emotional connection, maintaining open lines of communication, and supporting each other through difficult times. A resilient relationship is one that can withstand the ups and downs of life while continuing to move forward.

Practical Tip: Cultivate resilience in your relationship by practicing gratitude, maintaining a positive outlook, and focusing on your shared strengths. When faced with challenges, remind each other of the goals you've set and the progress you've made. This perspective helps you stay focused on the big picture and navigate obstacles with confidence.

Celebrating Milestones and Successes

As you work towards your long-term goals, it's important to celebrate the milestones and successes along the way. These celebrations reinforce your commitment to each other and provide an opportunity to reflect on your journey together.

7. Acknowledging Progress

Recognizing and celebrating your progress, no matter how small, keeps you motivated and reinforces the bond between you. It's not just about reaching the destination but also about enjoying the journey and the growth you experience together.

Practical Exercise: Set aside time to regularly reflect on your progress towards your long-term goals. Celebrate your achievements, discuss what's working well, and identify any areas that need adjustment. These reflections not only keep you on track but also deepen your connection as you acknowledge the efforts you've made together.

8. Reinforcing Your Shared Vision

Every success, big or small, reinforces your shared vision and strengthens your relationship. By celebrating these successes together, you build a sense of accomplishment and unity, making your long-term goals even more meaningful.

Practical Tip: Create rituals for celebrating your milestones, whether it's a special dinner, a weekend getaway, or simply taking a moment to express gratitude for each other. These rituals provide a tangible reminder of your commitment to each other and the future you're building together.

Reflective Questions

As you work on setting and achieving your long-term relationship goals, consider the following questions:

- » How well do our long-term goals align with our core values and joint aspirations?
- » Are there personal ambitions that need to be better integrated with our relationship goals?
- » How can we support each other's growth while working towards our shared vision?
- » What strategies can we use to navigate life's transitions while staying focused on our goals?
- » How can we celebrate our milestones and successes in a way that reinforces our shared vision?

Long-term relationship goals provide direction, purpose, and meaning to your journey together. By aligning your goals with your core values, balancing individual and joint aspirations, and navigating life's transitions with resilience and flexibility, you create a relationship that is both deeply connected and future-focused. Remember, the path to achieving these goals is a shared journey—one that requires ongoing communication, mutual support, and a commitment to your shared vision. With dedication and love, you can build a future that is as fulfilling as it is inspiring, together.

Foundations of an intimate relationship

At the heart of every successful intimate relationship lies a solid foundation—an unshakable base that supports the entire structure of your partnership. Just as a house cannot stand without a strong foundation, a relationship cannot thrive without the essential elements that create stability, trust, and love. This chapter explores the key components that form the bedrock of a lasting, fulfilling relationship, guiding you in building a connection that can withstand the test of time.

Trust: The Cornerstone of Intimacy

Trust is the cornerstone upon which all other aspects of a relationship are built. Without trust, the connection between partners remains fragile, easily disrupted by doubt and insecurity. Trust is not simply given; it is earned and maintained through consistent actions, honest communication, and a deep commitment to each other's well-being.

1. Building Trust Through Consistency

Consistency is key to building and maintaining trust. When your actions align with your words, and when you show up for your partner day after day, you create a sense of reliability that strengthens your bond. Trust is built through these everyday moments—by being there when you say you will be, by following through on promises, and by supporting your partner, especially in times of need.

Practical Exercise: Reflect on the ways you demonstrate consistency in your relationship. Are there areas where you could improve? Identify one action you can take this week to reinforce your reliability and strengthen the trust between you and your partner.

2. Honesty: The Foundation of Transparency

Honesty is the foundation of a transparent and open relationship. It involves being truthful not only in what you say but also in how you express your feelings, needs, and concerns. Honesty fosters a sense of safety in the relationship, allowing both partners to be their authentic selves without fear of judgment or rejection.

Practical Tip: Practice radical honesty in your relationship. Share your thoughts and feelings openly with your partner, even when it's difficult. Create a safe space where both of you can be honest without fear of negative consequences. This openness will deepen your connection and build a foundation of mutual respect and understanding.

Communication: The Lifeline of a Relationship

Effective communication is the lifeline that keeps a relationship vibrant and healthy. It's through communication that partners share their thoughts, feelings, and desires, resolving conflicts and deepening their understanding of each other. Without clear and open communication, even the strongest relationships can falter.

3. Active Listening: Truly Hearing Your Partner

Active listening is more than just hearing words; it's about fully engaging with your partner's message, both verbally and non-verbally. When you listen actively, you validate your partner's feelings, show empathy, and foster a deeper emotional connection.

Practical Exercise: During your next conversation with your partner, practice active listening. Focus entirely on what they are saying without interrupting or thinking about your response. Reflect back what you've heard to ensure understanding, and ask clarifying questions if needed. Notice how this practice enhances your communication and connection.

4. Expressing Yourself Clearly and Kindly

Clear and kind expression is essential for effective communication. It involves articulating your thoughts and feelings in a way that is both honest and respectful, ensuring that your partner understands your perspective without feeling attacked or criticized.

Practical Tip: Use "I" statements to express your feelings and needs. For example, instead of saying, "You never listen to me," try, "I feel unheard when I'm speaking, and I would appreciate it if we could work on our communication." This approach helps prevent defensiveness and fosters a more productive dialogue.

Respect: The Bedrock of Mutual Understanding

Respect is the bedrock of a healthy relationship. It involves honoring each other's individuality, values, and boundaries, even when you don't always agree. Respect is about seeing your partner as an equal, valuing their opinions, and treating them with kindness and consideration at all times.

5. Valuing Each Other's Differences

Every person is unique, with their own perspectives, experiences, and ways of being in the world. In a relationship, it's important to value these differences rather than seeing them as obstacles. By embracing each other's uniqueness, you create a relationship that is rich with diversity and mutual respect.

Practical Exercise: Take time to reflect on the ways in which you and your partner are different. How do these differences contribute to the richness of your relationship? Discuss with your partner how you can better appreciate and celebrate each other's individuality, strengthening the respect and understanding between you.

6. Setting and Respecting Boundaries

Boundaries are essential for maintaining a healthy relationship. They define what is acceptable and unacceptable behavior, protecting both partners' emotional and physical well-being. Respecting each other's boundaries is a fundamental act of love and consideration.

Practical Tip: Have an open conversation about boundaries with your partner. Discuss what boundaries are important to each of you and how you can respect them in your daily interactions. Revisit this conversation regularly to ensure that both partners feel safe, respected, and supported.

Commitment: The Glue That Holds It All Together

Commitment is the glue that holds a relationship together, especially during challenging times. It's the promise to stand by each other, to work through difficulties, and to keep the relationship a priority. Commitment is not just about staying together; it's about being fully invested in the well-being and growth of the relationship.

7. Demonstrating Commitment Through Action

Commitment is demonstrated through action—by showing up for your partner, making sacrifices when necessary, and continuously investing in the relationship. It's about choosing your partner every day, even when things get tough.

Practical Exercise: Reflect on the ways you demonstrate commitment in your relationship. Are there areas where you could be more present or supportive? Identify one specific action you can take this week to reinforce your commitment and show your partner that they are your priority.

8. Weathering Life's Storms Together

Every relationship will face challenges—whether it's external pressures, personal struggles, or conflicts within the relationship itself. How you navigate these storms together will determine the strength and longevity of your relationship.

Practical Tip: Approach challenges as a team, rather than as adversaries. Communicate openly about your fears and concerns, support each other through difficult times, and work together to find solutions. Remember, it's not the absence of challenges that defines a strong relationship, but how you handle them together.

Building a Lasting Foundation

The foundations of an intimate relationship are not built overnight; they require ongoing effort, dedication, and love. By prioritizing trust, communication, respect, and commitment, you create a relationship that is not only strong but also deeply fulfilling. These foundational elements are what will carry you through the ups and downs of life, allowing your relationship to thrive and grow stronger with each passing year.

Reflective Questions

As you work on building the foundations of your relationship, consider the following questions:

- » How strong is the trust between you and your partner?
- » What steps can you take to reinforce it?
- » Are there areas where your communication could be improved?
- » How can you practice better listening and clearer expression?
- » How do you show respect for your partner's individuality and boundaries?
- » Are there ways you could enhance this respect?
- » What does commitment look like in your relationship?
- » How can you demonstrate it more consistently?

The foundations of an intimate relationship are the key to its strength and longevity. By focusing on trust, communication, respect, and commitment, you create a relationship that is resilient, loving, and deeply connected. These elements are the building blocks of a partnership that not only endures but flourishes, providing both partners with the security, support, and joy they need to thrive. As you continue to nurture these foundations, you lay the groundwork for a relationship that will stand the test of time, growing ever stronger and more fulfilling as you journey through life together.

Conclusion

As we come to the close of this book, it's important to reflect on the journey you've embarked upon—a journey of growth, connection, and transformation. The principles, strategies, and insights shared throughout these chapters are not just tools for building a healthy relationship; they are the foundation for a life filled with love, trust, and mutual respect.

Embracing the Ongoing Journey

Relationships are dynamic, ever-evolving entities that require continuous nurturing and attention. There is no final destination, no point at which you can say, "We've arrived." Instead, the strength of your relationship lies in your ongoing commitment to each other and your willingness to grow together through life's many phases and challenges.

This journey involves embracing both the joys and the difficulties, understanding that each experience—whether positive or negative—offers an opportunity to deepen your connection. It's about celebrating the moments of triumph, learning from the moments of tension, and always striving to create a partnership that is resilient, supportive, and fulfilling.

Applying What You've Learned

Throughout this book, we've explored various aspects of building a thriving relationship—from communication and trust to financial planning and intimacy. As you move forward, the key is to apply these lessons in your daily life, making them an integral part of how you interact with your partner.

Communication: Continue to practice active listening and open dialogue, ensuring that both partners feel heard and understood. Communication is the lifeline of your relationship, and nurturing it will help you navigate both the calm and the stormy waters of life together.

Trust and Honesty: Keep building trust through consistent actions, vulnerability, and radical honesty. Trust is the bedrock upon which all other aspects of your relationship are built. Protect it, nurture it, and let it grow stronger with each passing day.

Conflict Management: Approach conflicts as opportunities for growth and understanding. Remember that the goal is not to win, but to resolve issues in a way that strengthens your bond and reinforces your mutual respect.

Intimacy: Cultivate both emotional and physical intimacy, recognizing that they are deeply interconnected. Prioritize your connection, make time for each other, and let your love continue to flourish in both new and familiar ways.

Balancing Space and Togetherness: Respect each other's need for personal space while cherishing the moments of togetherness. This balance is essential for maintaining a healthy relationship where both partners can grow individually and as a couple.

Long-Term Goals: Regularly revisit and refine your long-term goals, ensuring that they align with your evolving values and aspirations. A shared vision for the future is what keeps you moving forward together, united in purpose and love.

The Power of Reflection and Renewal

As you continue on this journey, take time to reflect on where you've been and where you're going. Reflection allows you to celebrate your successes, learn from your challenges, and recommit to your shared vision. Renewal comes from continually nurturing your relationship, finding new ways to connect, and keeping your love vibrant and alive.

Every relationship faces its own unique set of challenges and opportunities. What matters most is how you choose to navigate them—together. With the tools and insights from this book, you are well-equipped to create a relationship that not only endures but thrives.

Your Commitment to Each Other

In the end, the success of your relationship hinges on one thing: your commitment to each other. This commitment is not just about staying together; it's about being fully present, actively engaged, and deeply invested in your partner's happiness and well-being. It's about choosing each other every day, even when it's difficult, and finding joy in the shared journey.

Remember, the greatest relationships are those that are built on a foundation of love, trust, respect, and mutual growth. By applying the principles in this book, you are creating a relationship that honors both you and your partner—a relationship that is a source of strength, comfort, and joy for years to come.

Moving Forward Together

As you close this book, know that the journey doesn't end here. In fact, it's just beginning. Take what you've learned, apply it with intention, and continue to grow together as you move forward. The road ahead is filled with endless possibilities, and with each step, you have the opportunity to deepen your connection, strengthen your bond, and build a life that is rich with love and fulfillment.

May your relationship be one of lasting joy, unwavering support, and unbreakable connection. Together, you can achieve anything.

Continuing the Journey of Learning and Growth

Your relationship is a living, evolving entity that thrives on continuous learning and growth. Just as individuals grow and change over time, so too must your relationship. The more you invest in understanding each other, deepening your connection, and expanding your shared experiences, the stronger and more fulfilling your relationship will become.

Growth in a relationship is not about perfection but about progress. It's about recognizing that there is always more to learn—about yourself, your partner, and the dynamics between you. Embracing this journey with curiosity and openness allows you to navigate challenges with resilience and to celebrate your successes with genuine joy.

The Power of Lifelong Learning

Lifelong learning in a relationship means being committed to continual improvement and adaptation. It involves staying curious about your partner, seeking out new ways to connect, and being open to change. Whether it's exploring new interests together, deepening your emotional intimacy, or learning new communication skills, the pursuit of knowledge and growth will keep your relationship vibrant and strong.

Practical Tip: Make a habit of setting aside time to learn and grow together. This could involve reading books on relationships, attending workshops, or simply having regular conversations about how you can support each other's growth. By making learning a shared priority, you reinforce your commitment to each other and to the health of your relationship.

Embracing Change Together

Change is an inevitable part of life, and how you embrace it together will shape the future of your relationship. By being adaptable and open to new experiences, you create a dynamic partnership that can weather any storm. Growth often comes from stepping out of your comfort zone and facing challenges with a united front.

Practical Exercise: Identify one area of your relationship where you would like to grow or improve. This could be anything from communication to shared activities or even personal development goals. Work together to create a plan for how you can support each other in this area, and commit to revisiting your progress regularly.

Celebrating Growth and Progress

As you continue to learn and grow, it's important to acknowledge and celebrate the progress you've made. Every step forward, no matter how small, is a testament to your commitment to each other and your relationship. Celebrating these milestones reinforces the positive changes and motivates you to keep moving forward.

Practical Tip: Take time to reflect on the growth you've experienced as a couple. Celebrate your successes, discuss the lessons you've learned, and set new goals for the future. Whether it's a special date night, a weekend getaway, or simply a heartfelt conversation, these celebrations are a way to honor the journey you've taken together.

The Importance of Continuous Improvement

Continuous improvement is a key factor in maintaining a thriving relationship. This involves regularly checking in with each other to see how you're doing and making adjustments where necessary. It's not just about fixing problems but also about finding new ways to enhance your connection and understanding.

Practical Exercise: Schedule regular "relationship check-ins" where you discuss what's going well, what could be improved, and how you can support each other better. These check-ins are a proactive way to ensure that your relationship continues to grow and flourish.

The Journey Ahead

The journey of learning and growing in your relationship is ongoing, and it's one of the most rewarding aspects of a shared life. By staying committed to this journey, you build a relationship that is not only enduring but also rich in connection, understanding, and love. Remember, the greatest relationships are those that continue to evolve, adapt, and flourish over time. With each new chapter, you have the opportunity to deepen your bond, enrich your lives, and create a future filled with shared joy and fulfillment.

So, keep learning, keep growing, and keep nurturing the love that binds you together. The best is yet to come.

With heartfelt encouragement and best wishes,

Intimate Whispers